PUERTO RICAN PRINCESS

By: Shameca Walters

Copyright © 2024 by Seazons Collections Publishing House.

Copyright © 2024 by Scirocca Publication.

Copyright © 2024 by Shameca Walters.

All rights reserved. No part of this book may be reproduced or used in any manner without written permission of the copyright owner.

Dedication

Shout out to the Most High for allowing me this very moment. A special thanks to my A1's from day one. My best friend Angela Cabell Barker, my fiancé Carlos Garcia, my two siblings Thomas Coates, Roderick Walters, my baby girl Lakeysia Gadson, my dearest Oleatha Thurman and all of Grammy's Girls.

CONTENTS

Chapter 1	1
Chapter 2	5
Chapter 3	9
Chapter 4	12
Chapter 5	15
Chapter 6	19
Chapter 7	22
Chapter 8	26
Chapter 9	29
Chapter 10	32

Chapter 11	35
Chapter 12	38
Chapter 13	43
Chapter 14	47
Chapter 15	49
Chapter 16	53
Chapter 17	58
Chapter 18	61
Chapter 19	65
Chapter 20	69
Chapter 21	72
Chapter 22	75
Chapter 23	79
Chapter 24	83
Chapter 25	87
Chapter 26	93
Chapter 27	102
Chapter 28	109

Chapter 1

Who would have ever thought this would be the beginning of a whole new life for me. I was so upset today. We were moving from the sacred confines of my grandparents and I felt as if I was being torn apart. I really loved my grandparents. They didn't have lots of money but that never bothered us. We had unconditional love; that stuff that lasts for all those crazy days. The saddest part would be me enjoying the childhood that was about to be snatched away from me.

My mother knew that I was sad. She knew that I never wanted to leave my grandma. It was hot as hell outside and we had to carry all these boxes upstairs. I was evil and irate. All my mother was doing was getting on my damn nerves in real life. I could tell that this project complex was going to put it in my life. I never would have imagined that this would be the very place that molds my existence in the game.

The game was sold not told. I just looked at the people hustling and bustling in various directions. Little did I know at the time, they too were all chasing the bag. The same bag that fed families, yet kept us throwing bricks at the chain gang. This shit out here was realer than real Carver Estates; that's where I was bred.

My brothers were aggravating my soul that was something they took on at a very early age. I saw all the stares and glares of the neighbors. I wanted to say I was selfish because they were simply admiring my beauty. My father is Puerto Rican and my mother is African American. So, I am a stunning, slim built, yellow complexion, long, flowing, black hair beauty.

Carver Estates was the spot that everyone hung out at. There were so many apartments. There were family members living in the same complex. Then there were the friends and the friends of friends who knew people; so you know how that worked. No one ever slept. People were up during the wee hours of the morning. There would be niggas posted selling their products, there would be people selling merchandise big and small, then there were of course the chics that ran the projects checking for all the dope boys. The smaller boys would be on the back of the buildings shooting dice and gambling. Sometimes there were fights of rivals that lived in the same complex. Everyone knew everyone's business because there were always a set of eyes watching; even if they weren't visible to the naked eyes. Then there were times that we would go nigga knocking and run our asses off. When we did children things we always had fun, so we played around often.

Some days we would just sit on the meter box and talk about all types of stuff until we had to go inside. Then we would sit on the porch watching everything from the upstairs view. Once, my mom threw a party and she actually let me drink a wine cooler. It was so good and sweet.

Chapter 2

I loved my grandparents like none other because from as far back as I can remember, they were always the ones that provided for me when my mom was in need. We may not have had the best, but we had and that was what it was all about. My grandma spoiled me I was her only granddaughter. She took me on the weekends to the corner store. We used to shop there like it was Piggly Wiggly. But grandma didn't care that we had to pay higher prices, as long as we got what we wanted.

My grandparents didn't have a car so we walked everywhere we had to go or my grandma would pay someone to drive us around. My mom had a car and she would shop and do things for grandma when she wasn't working. My grandma was the best grandma in the whole world. She bathed me everyday and she tucked me in every night. Grandpa would teach me the Lords prayer and walk me to school. I had the best grandparents and I hated that we had to move away from them. I was the only child for about six years until my first brother came along and invaded my personal space. Grandpa would work every day and he would be off on the weekends; just hanging around the house drinking a few beers telling me story after story. All grandpa's stories were interesting. He told me all about his life growing up as a child and what it was like for him. I would just sit there listening and asking questions while grandma would be in the kitchen preparing our food.

Beauty has its pros and cons. There was the love and the hate involving jealousy that I possessed the precious gems within me, that allowed me to shine bright like a diamond. I never was the type to flaunt my possessions of course. I was pretty but I felt ugly at times; especially when I entered middle school and admired all of the big girls. Everyone hung with who they hung with and they were all dolled up. I was young but I sure wondered why they came to school each morning dressed date ready; makeup and all. I wish that my mom could afford to buy me the finer things or at least more things. I had clothes but they were always the cheap Flea Market, K-Mart, Walmart type stuff. Payless was the hottest shoe store around. Just because I wasn't well dressed, didn't change anything. I was beautiful inside and out. That alone made me special. Besides, we didn't compete around the hood because none of us had money like that to waste on material items. But the older chics that had the dope boys as boyfriends were always fly.

My mom used to always tell me it wasn't what I wore, it was how I wore it. Mama was old school to the core and she was one of a kind. Clothes mattered to me but I was pretty just like mama said. So whatever I wore, looked good. That's why them haters were hating.

Chapter 3

I loved the fact that I had long hair. It was all natural. I had been begging mama to let me get a Jerry Curl because the length of my hair would hold them curls so nicely. But mama wasn't going for it. She wanted me to remain a little girl as long as she lived; that's how she treated me. So getting any chemical products in my hair was dead. I had to rock the braids with the designs.

I sensed that there was a whole new world awaiting me around the corner because where we stayed with grandma, was small. This project was huge. It had buildings after buildings. So this was actually a world inside of a world. There were two playgrounds and they also had a basketball and football field. My brothers went to school right next to the office. Which was convenient for me since I was the one that took them to school and picked them up.

My mom was always working it seemed like it to me anyways. The best part about moving here was the store lady that had everything under the sun. It never was a dull moment around, so I should say we were just fine. My bad ass brothers already found them some lil bad ass friends; which was fine with me so I could catch a break. There was a girl that lived next door. She was ok so we hung out a little and played with our toys. I had thousands of barbies and all of the clothes, cars, and suitcases. We spent hours playing with dolls, dressing up and imagining a life far away from the ones we had. It was fun to do that because it made me feel so free.

My mom met this guy. They have been spending time together. I feel as if he has been around too long already. I didn't like him. There was something about him that didn't sit well with me. I just observed and said very little if anything at all. He wouldn't say much when my mom was around and I peeped that. So, I watched his ass.

Lo and behold, you know this low life pervert did his big one and got fresh with me. I wanted to tell my mom but I was afraid, I wondered if she would think I was lying trying to sabotage her relationship. This was why I thanked God for the friend I had met next door. She was the only person I had to tell. She couldn't believe what I was saying but it was the truth. I told my cousin. He was so cool. He hung out with all the fly guys that we wanted to be connected with. Plus, he didn't play. He would take a bitch down and I knew that. So, I told him about my mom's boyfriend.

Quite some time had passed since I told my cousin about what I was dealing with at home until I saw him again. I felt safe when he was around. I watched the way he carried himself. Nothing went past me unnoticed. I caught everything. I was sharp like that.

Chapter 4

My neighbors were all bad. We use to steal my moms car on the weekend when she would be getting wasted and take off. We needed a ride to the Palace. Which was the skating rink. We had so much fun on the weekends. I loved Saturday and Sunday. My dawg Spud was the truth. We used to chill everyday. He was so cute but I looked at him more like a lil brother. We did it all. Shopped, partied, and ate at expensive restaurants whenever we were together. I had been avoiding him because my mom was going to beat my ass if I took the car one more time. I was only twelve years old. But shit you couldn't tell me that I swore I was a little lady.

This particular weekend my mom went out. We went to mama Sarah's and got all the snacks in the whole world and just sat on the meter box in front of our building, clowning bitches all day. This was the shit we did on a daily. On the weekend we were always extra crunk. My mom's boyfriend was in the house. I wanted to avoid him at all costs.

My cousin was with me that day. "You're going in the house." He said.

"He's in there." I replied.

"Oh he is? I'd like to talk to him." He said with an evil look.

That was history because the talk ended with a beat down and he caught jack rabbit dodging them blows. My cousin was with a few of his homeboys. They stomped ole boy down like the dog he was and waited for my ole girl to come home so that he could tell her why he did what he did. I was actually shocked when she didn't lash out on me being at fault. With her, everything was my fault. I was held accountable for me and my brothers. That shit was so unfair. I was allowed to sleep over at certain friends. Sometimes, not all the time. I could have sleep overs as well. I found myself always looking for a way out but that didn't always work out for me.

Chapter 5

Shortly after the fight between my cousin and my mom's boyfriend. My mom and him separated. Which was great news being that I couldn't stand his ass. I'm so glad that my cousin was able to explain the situation to my mom. Once he did, she was all over ole boy and she wasn't letting him look sideways. I was just happy that he was finally gone so I wouldn't have to see his ass ever again.

In Carver Estates no one slept. People were up and out all throughout the night; just as they were during the day. The boosters would come through with gear, the freshest shit off the market for the low-low. Pretty much you can find anything you wanted. Just sit on the bench in the middle of the building and the people would just come. The niggas on the back side are always gambling and selling drugs. That's the side that my mom said she didn't want me on. But you know me being grown and fast, I went anyways. All the fine niggas were around there dressed up. Fly kicks, good smelling cologne, loud music from their loud cars, big whips and lots of chips. The older girls in this complex were walking around acting as if they ran shit.

One of the dope boys always looked at me a certain way and I loved when he did that. I never said anything, but of course one day he said something to me. I smiled from ear to ear. He even brought me something from the ice cream truck. It was all good though. I definitely thought he was or possibly could be the one. I couldn't mess with no lame. Now that just wasn't my style. I was fly so I had to have a fly guy to match my level of ego. That's how I saw it. Simple! I mean what could a scrub do for me? He better not even look my way. I wasn't materialistic. Hell, I didn't even have a boyfriend. I just saw things the way I saw them. So, that's how I moved.

I never knew that the dope boy that had caught my eye had a girlfriend. She did not like me. Why would this teenage girl stare at me and roll her eyes? I don't know her and I don't want any problems. I wasn't slow by far. I saw how she shot mugs at me for no apparent reason she must've found out that I was talking to her ex. I was never going to say anything about him unless she asked me. In my mind I felt that if she was ever bold enough to step to me, I would be bold enough to kick her ass. See these hoes around here, they would try a bitch if she let them. But one thing my mom didn't raise, was a punk. I would fight and fight until I couldn't fight anymore. About me, any bitch can get it. I wasn't a fighter. That was a far cry from the person I really am. But sometimes a bitch will try us. As the elders say, "Respect is not given, it is earned.

I will be happy when my friend comes back next

door so I can tell her about the evil looks I been receiving from the chic about her dude. My friend was older. So she wasn't afraid to step to that hoe and be like, "Bitch, what you eyeing my dawg for? We got a problem!" Straight like that. In that order! I was confused. Did she want smoke?

Chapter 6

It was just an average day around the way when all of a sudden my mom came home early from work. One thing my mom did was work. She did her thang when she wanted to; don't get me wrong. But she was a damn good provider. She was a single mother of three. We all had different fathers, so the sole responsibility was hers. She did her very best to take care of us by any means necessary. That's another reason I loved her so much. Even when she was mean to me, I still loved her. I can't remember one time I loved her any less.

My mom wasn't feeling well. So, I had to help

take care of her. This went on over the next few days or so until she finally said she was in so much pain she couldn't take it anymore. She called the ambulance. This would be the day that would forever change my life. She was admitted and she wasn't released until two days later. My aunt arrived at the hospital and informed me and my brothers that she would be staying with us until our mom came home.

At that point everything spiraled out of control and I'm talking in a major way. My mother was diagnosed with HIV. That changed the course of my life for all my days to come. I never remember seeing my grandma cry and she was hard down crying; slanging snot. I had no clue what HIV was and I most certainly didn't know that I would end up losing my mom. Things were fragile to say because me and my brothers were sad that our mom was sick and she couldn't take care of herself or us.

My aunt is the love of my life. Never once did she think twice about sacrificing her very own life to give it for her sister. One thing about our family, we are all we got. We love each other and we are as thick as thieves when it involves one of us. That's the way family is supposed to be. I see so many families are broken and distant, due to their own selfish reasons. We weren't like that. We are the complete opposite. It was a lot easier with my aunt being the head of the house temporarily. She was much more nicer than mom.

I started to cry when I would hear my mom crying out to my aunt in pain and delusion. That hurt me to my heart. I couldn't bear the sight of my mother suffering and there not being anything I can do about it. If I never felt hopeless, it was then at that moment I realized this wasn't good. It was only getting worse. I needed time to breathe outside of my current environment. So, I began hanging out a little later than I normally would. I had so much on my mind. It was as if I was carrying around the weight of the world. Should I say that's not a good feeling? I felt like my world was coming to an end. It was collapsing all around and I'm becoming closed in…..

Chapter 7

No matter how much pain I felt, I knew from that day on I could never give up. I must give it my all until I can't go another round. Life will knock us down if we allow it. We must get back up and push harder. This is the time that my strength, determination, and courage takes over.

My aunt never talked about my mom situation. She loved her sister and now she was faced with raising three children on her own. Over the span of the next year or so, things at home were still crazy. I floated around from one spot to the other you know. I met some real good people along the way who really embraced me and the circumstances surrounding me. I asked my aunt if she would rent me a place. A little duck off that could keep me safe. Of course she did. So now I stayed away longer periods than I normally did because I couldn't deal with my mom's condition.

I was bored to death this day and I couldn't concentrate on anything. Everything was foggy. I went and used the bathroom and as I sat there, something came over me and said, "Go and see your mom." I showered and threw on a short set and some tennis shoes and hit the pavement. I walked all the way to the hospital; which may have been approximately 3/4 of a mile. Once I got off the elevator and headed towards my mom room, I was in disbelief when the whole room was empty. I flew over to the nurse station.

"Excuse me. My mom was in room 324. Where is she?" I asked.

The nurse said sympathetically, "You should contact your family members. Your mother has been moved to hospice."

I'm like what is hospice and where the fuck is my mom? I literally ran home. That's how fast I got there. My aunt told me that we would go in the morning to see my mom. All that was on my mind was my mom. How was I going to sleep tonight. It was the longest night ever. I must've smoked a thousand joints and still no sleep.

When morning came, I was already ready pacing the floor waiting to find out what the hell was going on. I wanted to know why my ole girl couldn't come home. Somebody was going to tell me something and that was for sure. What seemed like an eternity became reality when my aunt arrived. She had my grandparents with her. We all drove to hospice to see my mom. That was a long ass ride. The whole car ride there, I was lost so deep in thought. Why was any of this happening to me? I was just a little girl that wanted to be a little girl. But everyday things leaned more and more towards me growing up asap.

My mom was laying in that damn hospital bed looking like a vegetable. I hated this shit. It was eating me alive. The core of my bones ached and there was an excruciating pain that tore clean through me. I was hurt, sad, and numb at the same damn time. It was too hard to watch my ole girl lay there helplessly; knowing that there wasn't a damn thing that I could do to save her. All I wanted was to make the situation better for my whole family; especially my brothers. If I was hurting so bad, I can only imagine the pain they felt.

The few moments that me and my ole girl shared were our last moments together in this lifetime. Those memories are forever etched within the lining of my heart. Later that night, she passed away. At least she wasn't suffering no more. In my mind I felt like she was in a better place now.

Chapter 8

My grandparents planned the funeral and this was when I spent more time with my grandma. She was already old. Although she had minor health problems, I just felt the urge to love her more. Now I knew that life was truly a gift because the same life we love to live and live to love, can be gone in the blink of an eye.

My aunt was holding herself up well. She wasn't drinking her norm because boy could she take them back and get litty. The only thing she did was drink, talk shit, and make you laugh. She was really my best friend. She always comforted me since the day

I entered this world. That's my girl.

Our immediate family of course showed up and supported us during our time of bereavement. That made it all that much easier for me to deal with. I tried to block out the times she would come in the door and pick us up. Myself, her, and the boys would ride. The small things like me being sick, or afraid of something. My mom was my protector. She would die a million times over about me. I was her only daughter. Even though I'm sad, I will thrive every day of my life to carry her legacy within me. So to me, she still lives through me.

This brought me and my aunt closer. I also gained the freedom I so wanted when my mom was alive. My main concern and total focus was now my brothers who needed me now more than anything. After all, my aunt didn't work. She was a stay at home wife. She had us now. So she collected social security benefits for us until we got eighteen years old. That still wasn't much being that she had to pay the bills, provide food for us to eat, clothes and every other necessity we had. This shit was too real.

I had to do something. I needed some cash quick and fast.

Chapter 9

I hadn't been to school since God knows when. When my mom fell down bad, I gave up everything and got lost. Just that more as if drowning in my own pain, swimming in my own misery. I had met a friend that lived outside of the gate and we spent a lot of time hanging out. Her mom and dad were still together. They all lived together and they always made me feel at home. So that became my home away from home.

Over there where she lives, there was a lot going on also. They had their set of street niggas that ran that block and it was never boring over there. She had an older brother. So him and his friends were always around. We would laugh at them and we would also make them buy us anything that we wanted. We had so much fun. She wasn't into the things that I was into. But that never came between our friendship. We were always together even though we were like night and day. We became friends forever.

It was almost as if I got lost within the feelings that were surreal to me. The pain was just insurmountable and I was barely getting by. Pretending that everything would be ok and I would be able to live life happily ever after. Well sorry! Not in this book! This was a book about hard knocks that transformed themselves into the thoroghbred's they were. There are no bragging rights when money don't mean shit in a world where you lose everything you have. Watching it being snatched away right before your very eyes. Then we wonder how we got to the point that we at right now.

The streets that I ran in were cold and

calculated. Around every corner, there were predators lying in wait to devour the innocent child that sees a way out. The world was structured to make one believe that they were the ones in control. When in all actuality, they were only deceiving themselves of becoming who they really could be. This shit was at an all time low. I just felt as if I had given my very all and still gained nothing. That was the place where I was and no one could change how I felt.

I often felt that the walls were closing down on me and there was absolutely nothing that I could do about it. Since my mom passed, all I really had was my auntie. She damn sure made sure we may have been different from the other folks but at the end of the day, we were all we had. We damn sure made a bitch recognize us.

Life had changed so fast and suddenly. I was once a little girl enjoying life and then I was stripped down naked of the girl that was lost inside of this hard shell, we put on to protect us when it's really harming us.

Chapter 10

In the funky ghetto, we had nothing more to look forward to than a Saturday or Sunday at a group home where we are stranded miles on top of miles away from civilization. While being closely monitored by them white folks. Do we recall the times we were at the phone booth placing operator assisted long distance calls, billing to the telephones actual owner and we never stopped there. We would even go to the extent of conducting emergency break throughs. These sure were the good ole days and I would definitely be seizing every opportunity that's allowed to me. After all, we weren't offered anything in this world. We had to take what we believed to be ours and fight for what we wanted. Everyday was a struggle. In my mind, this was only the beginning.

God said in the bible, He was the alpha and omega. The beginning and the ending. Some things in life could only appear in the form of lessons because sometimes we have to experience things to bring us to our full capacity whatever that may be.

Things became so fierce that I started drinking and I admit, I never for saw me being an alcoholic. But that was the person I slowly started turning into. The most sad part was that I recognized it. It was like after mom died, I just gave up and my fight became less weaken. It was cool to do whatever we wanted to do and we never gave any thought, care, or concern, to anything or anyone other than that. I had been trying to do my best and remain as strong as I could. When there were still times that I gave up and had to rely upon the inner strength of my family. I felt so helpless and hopeless. In their eyes I probably looked like a whole idiot. Nevertheless,

I was me and I didn't give three fucks about a bitch because I paid my own way. Now that my ole girl was gone, I had to maintain by any means.

My auntie and I really got close. We were all each other had and in our eyes. We were able to look past the bull shit; blood thicker. Plenty nights I got sad and cried myself to sleep while consuming an alcoholic beverage to calm me down. Although I knew this wasn't the answer, I knew that I was weak and heavy laden.

Chapter 11

On that side of town, I can make some plays that can help me out financially and give me that boost to get on my feet. She would always say, "Cuz be careful." She still says that to this very day. Some days were better than others. Some days my aunt would drink herself into a coma and then there were days she was focused. I never could understand why she acted so strange. She was hurting inside too. So, she was crying out. Her beer, liquor, or wine was her escape. We all wanted to escape the jungle. I know I did and there was nothing that would stop me from getting out someday.

I dreamed that early on in life that my destiny was full of adventure and I was equipped already with the courage of a lion to risk on leaps of faith. I can't lie and say that we went to church regularly. It wasn't until my mom got sick that we became involved in the church community. My mom had some friends that helped her out and of course they were God fearing people. I recall a few occasions when me and my grandma would attend church services when I spent some weekends with her. Her church was filled with the Holy Ghost. That's what grandma would say. I never understood, so I would just look on.

All grandma did when ma died was sit on her neighbors porch and talk with them all day long. I would help her out. Each time I stopped by, I would bless her pockets so she could get whatever she needed. I had a room at my grandparents house the entire time we moved away and I was free to come and go when I needed to. I was always blessed to be in the presence of my grandparents; both alive and well. Old? Yes! But hey, they are still together. Been married for years; my mom was the baby. They got married when they had her. She was 30 when she died. So they have been married well over 30 years.

That's the type of man I want. One just like my grandpa. He did everything that a man was supposed to do to take care of his family and he didn't resort to the streets. He worked hard every day. When he had a car, he drove. When he had to walk, he walked. Either way, nothing stopped him and we made it. His perseverance was extremely strong and I thank God that I am blessed with that same bloodline.

Chapter 12

It was as if I no longer existed. I fell into a state of heavy depression. I probably would have been legally intolerant and incapable. It was like my spirit was so broken. I felt so empty inside. There was a huge pot hole that I seemed to be sinking away in. After mom's death, I basically gave up sort of because the fact of dealing with her death being forever gone was eating me alive. I wouldn't go no where. All I did was stay inside the house smoking and drinking. Back then drinking was just something we did around the hood when we wanted to be in a comatose state. That's exactly where I wanted to be.

My home girl was checking for me because I shut down and isolated myself from the world. It was like I was trying to run away in my mind. I never drunk so much. All I had been doing was getting wasted. Shit there wasn't anything else to do. I had completely lost all hopes of becoming interested in school again. I was a child by age; don't get me wrong. But I was also a woman. A mini woman that had an S on her chest. That was my motto. But after I lost my ole girl, I found less interest in life itself. It's sad that another human being can bring us so much pain. I needed to get my hair done. I needed to go to the salon and get the works; manicure, pedicure, fill, eyebrows, and lashes. But what the fuck for? Who was I looking for. My mom....definitely not a nigga.

This trauma was unbearable. I spent completely out of control. I tried to realize that there wasn't nothing I could ever do to bring back my ole girl. So I had to be strong. But there were many days and many nights that I spent reminiscing on the special memories embedded in my heart. Here it is I am fourteen years old and I have no mother. My aunt began to worry about me because I wasn't holding up too well. She wanted me to seek psychiatric treatment. But why? Was I crazy is what I wanted to know.

Things weren't getting any better so I decided to utilize the different programs and agencies that were available to me and my brothers. Besides, maybe I did need help. I never could understand how someone else can tell me the answers to my problems. But these white folks have it set for a person to think that. I didn't look at it right at that moment about being black or white. It was about me. I needed some help. At first I felt odd telling a person my personal business. I feel like a person could be judge mental of one, just based on their race and income. I wasn't ashamed of who I was nor where I came from. I am who I am.

Therapy soothed the pain somewhat. I enjoyed being able to be open up with others about what I experienced. If any of them had a heart, they would have empathy for me. Being a parent, I couldn't imagine losing a child. So me being just a child who lost her mom, how did anyone think I felt or did anyone even care?

It's a cold world out here in these streets that we call the concrete jungle. I was getting firsthand preparation. Hard-knocks 101. My therapist felt that I was capable of dealing with the five stages of grief. I actually felt that way too. It's just that everything pretty much happened fast. Which left me to numb the pain. It was too much to deal with all at once. It's going to take time for me to regain myself and my mind. All my friends were very caring. They didn't want me to waddle in the mud. They wanted me to bounce back. But that was the strangest shit. All of them had their moms, so how did they know how I felt?

Regardless of how I felt, I knew I had to be strong for my brothers because they were looking up to me. I never wanted to be viewed as a failure or let down. We just lost our moms. So now that we only had each other, we all became overprotective of our love.

Chapter 13

This is where my character was designed. I was built ford tough, and energizer bunny built to last. Any other normal child was not going through any of the shit. But I was. Did that make me un normal? Why did it seem as if all of the odds were against me?

Hell, I ain't pick this hand I was dealt it. Over time, I got back in the groove of things and that's when I noticed that it was now my aunt breaking down. That's how death does you because one minute you're perfectly fine and then you're totally saddened. I felt my aunt pain. Hell, she was a grown ass lady and she was showing her heart. She was crying out. That shit hurts deep like a cut to the gristle. I sat there and paid attention and she drunk all day long; one right behind the other. She was falling off. She began to take the checks we got from social security and drink them up to. She stayed down there crediting from Mama Sarah. I was mad as hell. How dare she take the money that my mom worked hard for and drink it up! Not to mention, the money was to take care of me and my brothers and she was taking care of herself.

I was so embarrassed when people came over. We had raggedy furniture and we never had real groceries. This was a huge problem for me and my aunt. I have to stop her or at least try at this point. She is on the verge of drinking her life away. "Auntie, I need to talk to you about the checks coming on the third."

She flew around so damn fast. Damn near losing her footing. "Fuck you! You red bitch! I know your brothers done went and got you!" She said.

"Auntie, please stop now. I don't want to fight

you."

I guess that I will say that was our first physical altercation. She had been drinking and of course I love her. I would never harm her intentionally. But damn she can't harm me either. It's like when she be drinking, she turn into someone completely insane. She would get so angry that she would do loud outburst and say some of the craziest shit you ever heard. Guess what? She be dead ass serious. I had to make time to see my grandmother about auntie drinking because she couldn't continue drinking up the money. We've always had a perfect relationship. But since mom died, it's like we were always at each other's neck. Yeah, I'm on her ass because she has to do right by us.

I may be small in the laws eyes but I'm an adult when it concerns the boys and she knew that. If she didn't, she does now.

I went and stayed at home for the weekend so me and my grandma could have a long talk about how auntie was handling things. I didn't mean to be a snitch. I had to say something though. I waited until that night before I sparked up the conversation with grandma and she listened to every word I said. That's why I loved her. She was my girl. "All we can do is go down to the social security place and change the payee to me so I can disburse the funds." She said.

"That's a great plan grandma." I said.

That Monday, we went down there and did the paperwork so that the change could go into effect immediately. She wasn't going to be happy about this move that me and grandma made in silence. But it's her fault. She left me no choice. All she wanted to do was argue with me and fight me for telling her what's right. She a grown woman. She done seen way more than I have and she damn sure should be smarter than me.

Chapter 14

In the mean time, all I did was pick back up the pieces of my broken life. As soon as auntie found out what me and grandma did, she was pissed. She talked shit to me. If she would have disrespected my grandma, I was going to take her ass down.

My grandma was older now and she had problems with her leg. So I always did whatever I could so she would be straight. If she needed anything I had her and even when I didn't have it, I went to get it about her.

It was so peaceful at grandma's. I kept my room clean and neat bed made at all times. I loaded my walls with pictures of my mom. I wanted to look at her everyday for the rest of my life. I did all the cleaning for my grandparents so that their place was clean. The bathroom was immaculate. I did all of the grocery shopping for her so she didn't have to worry.

Sometimes we would just sit around and order fast food and watch movies; talking until we fall asleep. I had me a window ac installed in my bedroom because my grandma was straight old fashion and she loved for it to be hot. It was too damn hot for the bullshit. Now that I did that, grandma said she wanted me to pay the light bill. Whatever to make her happy.

Chapter 15

Me and my friends all we did was steal. It became a bad habit that was formed at an early age. The very first time I shoplifted was with my home girl. She picked me up and we was riding, chilling and she said she had to go to the store. She went inside there and took the people down. I was shocked as fuck to see her pull all them sweat suites out that purse. OMG!!! This was the lick and I was on the play. I went into the next store and I took them down too.

Everyday we would make $600. That was a lot of money to make from stealing clothes in one day.

Puerto Rican Princess

We did this on a regular and the money was coming faster than the product. We had orders to fill, so much clientele and we did not have enough time. This was a plus for me because of the boys. Now they were able to wear the name brand designer clothes that mom couldn't afford to buy us because my mom wasn't buying no damn Sanders, Barkley's, or Hitachi's. And it was evident that the only thing auntie was buying was alcohol by the boat loads every chance she could. I know that stealing is wrong but does it make it right that I have no other choice but to take it. I wasn't born with a silver spoon in my mouth. I was born in the ghetto. My brothers were so happy they had all the shoes and all the clothes. They were happy at least from the outside looking in because the inside looking out was shattered. As long as I could put a smile on their faces, I was good and that's how we roll pretty much.

Every thang was every thang and everybody was doing them. Whatever them consisted of. We had so many damn clothes. We never ever wore the same outfit twice. That's when I accumulated a large bill at the cleaners to keep my gear fly.

I became more popular now that I had started moving things as I called it. I loved to hang out with my friends older sister. She was so cool and everyone respected her and when we went out, we always had a good time. I'm talking about going out to the club shaking our booty type shit. That's what we was on. She had lots of boyfriends. I admired her. I said when I grow up, I want to be just like her. I want all the men flocking at my feet. That was so damn sexy to me. Don't get me wrong, I had a flock of niggas on go, but they were so lame to me. If I will because never did I want the ones that were financially able to provide for me. I wanted the ratchet ones that want to play cat and mouse games. I didn't have a steady boyfriend that was something I couldn't get into because if a nigga wanted to be with me, he was gone damn sure pay like he way. See I was different from the rest of them hoes from the gate because I never wanted a nigga to take care of me. I took care of my damn self by any means necessary and that's how I looked at relationships.

Half of these niggas ain't worth the time of day because all they do is lie to get pussy. While all the while getting caught up in the shit. I couldn't. I had just went through way too much pain to even consider a relationship. I loved being single. It allowed great freedom to do whatever I wanted. I was trying to make money during the day not chase niggas. They knew with me it was never going to be easy because I'm a lil girl for real that's making more money than them and they stand on the street corners all day. Pathetic in real life. When I did get a nigga, everyone would definitely know. It will be on display for all to see.

Chapter 16

Delray wasn't big enough for me or either I was too big for Delray. We were a lil city but we definitely on the map. Atlantic Ave. Exit 12, I-95. We partied hard Delray style, 'Telray,' we hung on the Ave where everyone who was somebody hung. The Ave was always thick and we brought the whole city and surrounding cities out. The Dirty Nine which was a street off the Ave, directly in the midst of things. I was young but hey, I was on every scene. I hung with all the older chics and barely often my real friends. I guess I was seeking the direction of the old heads because they maneuvered the streets thoroughly. I, myself just was into having fun. We walked to the beach, we went to the pool, and we spent time clicked up. We ran deep and trust me them hoes wanted no smoke. I was still learning everything and transforming into a young woman. I was becoming more interested in sex. I had never thought much about it until I started hanging with my sisters; I called them.

Delray was so small. Everyone knew everyone. So they said that my mom was messing with a man that was married with a whole family. I just took to them because they were such sweet people. They were a big family. There were four girls and one boy. I used to dream of having a family that was large or at least a big sister. In my world I was the one and only sister. I kind of started crushing on their brother being that I was there every weekend. He acted as if I didn't even exist. I did so many things trying to gain his attention. One of his big sisters was my best big sister. She was so nice to me. She took me under her wings and showed me the womanly things I had no knowledge of. She was the person who taught me how to insert a tampon.

I watched the older girls so I could see how to be like them. They were all pretty. It's like they could possibly be my sisters; we actually did favor. The last thing I wanted was for us to be family because I couldn't date my brother. I was fourteen and still a virgin. I'm feeling this nigga so I might as well give him my virginity and let him pop my cherry. I wanted to do it so badly but I was so afraid it made me nervous just thinking about sex.

Once he knew that I was feeling him, he ran with it. See this the shit I be talking bout. The games that people play.

One night on the weekend, he sent his little sister to tell me he wanted me. He was in his room laying on his bed. I opened the room door and stuck my head in. "Whats up?"

"You." He stated. "Come in." I was so happy that he acknowledged me but what did he want me to come in the room alone with him for? I sat on the edge of the bed and he started telling me all this bullshit that sounded real good at the time to lure me into his bed. He could sense the nervousness or uneasiness because I was so scared. He grabbed my hands and pulled me into him. When I got close enough, he grabbed my ponytail and held the back of my head, while slowly tongue kissing me. I was moist at the thought of the first kiss. He certainly didn't stop there. He got off the bed, laid me down and penetrated me deep within. It was so sad because I can't say that I enjoyed it. It was an experience that left no feeling. After we had sex of course I bled some. I was like shit why am I bleeding?

We messed around off and on for a few months until I decided I had enough. After he had sex with me, he treated me like a dog and acted as if he was embarrassed by me liking him. I used to get so sad and hurt. I never felt good enough or pretty enough. I would cry because he made me think that there was something wrong with me. I had to shake him off and get over him so I stopped going over hanging like I used to. Eventually, we both forgot about each other.

At first, I was hurt. But I ended up realizing that I had no clue about what love really was. Here I was thinking I loved him when I didn't even like him. I regret having sex with him because he destroyed the bond that I had with my sisters who were his sisters. It took some time for me to get him completely out of my system and go unbothered by his actions. I never told too many people about him and the only people that knew were the ones that were around us. I never could understand what he didn't like about me? Why wasn't he into me the way I was into him? Did he just plan to pretend to like me? Those were some of the things that crossed my mind. But at the end of the day, I couldn't let him get the best of me. If for some reason he felt I wasn't pretty enough that's his bad because I knew I was beautiful. He tried his best to make me jealous. When I did pop up he was into another girl that was no where near as pretty as me. But he was loving him some her. I acted like I wasn't phased when all the while I felt like the laughing stock of the crowd. I made a mental note to never come back around again.

Chapter 17

Since I was back in Carver Estates I networked with my home girls and we lined some shit up to make a play at the new mall. I had to have them new handbags. Them Dooney Bourkes was the shit and I had damn near everyone that was out. I was about my coins but when it came down to certain stuff, I had to have it. My vision became clearer and I had actually put some thought into maybe going back to school. I wanted to get my GED. I dropped out of school in the ninth grade and why? I still can't figure because I was an honor roll student. When I hit high school, everything went out the window.

My aunt had been telling me to go back to school and I really was considering it.

Monday morning I went to the adult education center and enrolled for GED school and signed up for the next available test; which was approximately two months away. That left me with work to do. I had to prepare for the test so I devoted my undivided attention to school. I put all the hustling to the side and did my big one. I studied so long and so hard, it was unreal. On my way to take the test, I was reading my notes. I wanted to make sure that I forgot nothing. Once the test was complete, I had to wait a few months for the results. I had no doubts that I aced it. Now I just had to wait to see; only time will tell.

I was laying in my bed watching BET when my brother yelled. "Sis you got mail."

"From who?"

"I don't know. It's a big yellow envelope from the board of education."

I jumped off my bed and ran in the living room and grabbed my mail. Once I tore it open, the very first sentence said, congratulations. Everything after that didn't matter. I was so proud of myself. Now I was an actual high school graduate. Ain't God good!!!! I stayed encouraging my brothers to do the very best that they can. That was an understatement because of our circumstances. I never wanted them to be at them low dark places that kept me. At least now when they say their sister dropped out of school, they can say she went back and graduated.

None of my friends were really happy for me because where we came from, school was the last thing we worried about. Only the children discussed school. I feel like a lack of education can make one ignorant and Lord knows I never want to labeled as an idiot.

Chapter 18

My cousin, baby mama came by and told me she needed to holler at me. So we chopped it up briefly. She told me that she had a new play for us to run, was I in. I said hell yeah. See these girls respected me because I had way more heart than them. It was like I was a nigga letting my nuts hang. I ain't have no point to prove. I had to get what was mine. That's all it was. Simple for me. Life for me was great or shall I say, better than it was considering the factors I been dealing with. All I did was smoke weed and hang with the girls. We always had a good time and it was so peaceful until a bitch would get out of line and it would go digital.

All my dawgs was on go and they really didn't have issues too much because a bitch knew they had to bring it fucking with them. As for me, I was the total opposite. Don't get me wrong, we would keep haters no doubt. But me, I was on the pretty girl type shit like I ain't got no time for that. I figured if it ain't make money, it damn sure ain't make sense. Lots of hoes around my way hated the fact that their baby daddies wanted a piece of this red velvet cake. Pitiful, them hoes are they can keep them niggas and they problems. All I want is the head and the bread. Shit I got to play them before they play me. One thing about it, Ruth ain't raise no fool and they can bet they bottom dollar on that.

The paradise was jumping tonight. That shit swung until the early morning hours. Keeping troll on deck because it could pop off at any given. That's how it went down where I am from. We carried. There was never a dull moment in Delray. I liked the club down on 6th Ave.. It was more laid back and the age group was more of my caliber. Shit the

Dice wouldn't let you in without ID and we all knew I wasn't old enough to have my ass in there. I slid a couple times but that wasn't my crowd. They were too grown and sexy for me. I loved some hood shit. The disc jokey kept it coming. He was a beast on the turn table. He had the whole club rocking; making a bitch think they could actually get up on a room. Every time I went to the Amber House, the DJ would always dedicate a song to me and give me a shot out. He called me yellow child and he would say this here goes out to yellow child. Then that R Kelly would drop. "Temperatures rising and your bodies yearning." Oh yeah we were on one. Of course we all had caught some niggas to duck off with. So before we would head to the room, we would stop at Wags and get some food to go, off to the room to smoke, eat, and fuck all night. Them anyways because a nigga wasn't going to trick me out my panties. He would have a hell of lot more to do for me then get me a room. It wasn't even a room it was a suite at the Residence Inn Marriott. It was straight and all but boss niggas never needed their home boys to chip on a room. Want to impress me, buy me a car nigga or get me a crib and put it in my life.

Chapter 19

Lately, I noticed I had been feeling heartless and that was scary because that wasn't even my character. I guess that's what the streets do to you. That's what it did to me.

Finally, I made time to catch up with Cuz. She had waited to see me, so she could check up on me. She and I were close and we confided and shared with each other the things that we couldn't tell anyone. She was always on the up and up. I was the complete opposite. Which it still worked. I guess that's where our friendship had balance. Nevertheless, it was always love with Cuz and I.

Puerto Rican Princess

When I got to Cuz, she was still laying down, watching TV. Which was cool. It gave us time without the interruptions to chop it up. Cuz wanted to go to nursing school. She was trying to get me to enroll in the class with her but I didn't want to do that. Here it is, I'm fifteen years old. I can't say that I want to be a nurse. I mean nurses are wonderful people. They are the ones that take care of us and our families. But I don't feel like that's my calling. I feel Cuz though. Get that trade under your belt and shit get that check. But for me, money came fast because of the lifestyle I lived. Me and Cuz operated totally different so she couldn't understand me and I couldn't understand her. So we just talked about other things.

We both had a lot going on but she had more family structure. That's really the real reason I stayed at Cuz often. I loved the love from her and her family. I had a new family from the outside world. I guess I am special because I ended up being friendly with a few people. Hey, I said a few not to many.

I felt Cuz though. She was concerned about me and she wanted me to make better choices. But the point in my life where I was, I couldn't do that if I wanted to. My home girls that I hustled with were planning to stunt. So I had to get in on that to at least see what the play really was. I hit them up and they slid through. Man they was loaded. Them hoes had everything under the sun. All the flyest shit. I was like, "Well damn. Y'all could've hit me up and let me run up a check."

Sometimes I feel as if there's a reason why I handled them the way I did with a long handle spoon. I guess grandma was right you got to keep your enemies close and watch your homies. This type of shit made me want to reconsider my options and reevaluate my environment. There were so many things running through my head because my grandma had been stressing me lately too. She ain't want me stealing. She knew I wasn't buying the things I had.

We had finally got the insurance money from our mom policy. Grandma went and opened up each of us a bank account. So she probably figured why the hell is my granddaughter doing this dumb shit. As much as I love her, she would never be able to understand the life I live. That made me feel bad deep down inside because my family needed me so I couldn't make mistakes that would land me in a bad situation. I had too many people depending on me. I couldn't fail. That's all I told myself over and over again.

Chapter 20

This shit ain't never stopped. Everyday it was the same old thing. Chase a dollar. We were always on the plot to come up. As crazy as it seems, we always made a dollar out of fifteen cents. See my crew, we hustled hard. Ain't that's what we were supposed to do? If we play hard, we have no other option; hustle harder. We out hustled them average niggas. We made real moves in that order.

Never could I have imagined that I was becoming equipped with the knowledge, wisdom, and credibility required to reign in these streets. The streets really have a life of its very own. They showed me how to survive in any type of situation; whether the obstacles are small or great.

Over the years I mastered street life of survival to the fittest. I learned many schemes to make a dollar. My mama always did say there was more than one way to skin the cat. The only thing we chase is that we strive every day with a true hustler's ambition. Having faith and believing that anything that God brings us to, he will most certainly bring us through. For some apparent reason, I thought about my mom heavy today. It made me feel like it was the coldest winter ever. My brothers were getting big now so they always wanted to dress nice or maybe it was always me that wanted them to look a certain way. Who would have ever thought that we would overcome as many painful obstacles in life as we did.

Now it seemed as if it was all on me. So I had to carry the weight of my world on my back. I had run into a few people that were into some real money–making plays. I had to link up with them to get that bread. Little did I know the game was sold never told. Behind each mission there were serious repercussions. But at this point in my life, I felt as if I had everything to gain and nothing to lose. I did what I did to take care of me and mines. When the bumps in the road appeared, I just strapped down for the ride. My motive everyday was money, money, and more money.

After all, what else was there to do? I wasn't attending school, so out the window went education. I had to make boss moves. Everything was pretty much everything. By this time the daily hustle and bustle of our complex was at a high capacity. So there was practically everything under the sun going down in on projects. We all were in poverty and with that being said, we were definitely poverty stricken. The struggle was at an all times high. There was basers copping dope, niggas doing the most, and hoes straight swerving. It seems as if everyone was in their own world just doing what they had to in order to survive. Times were at an all time low but we have had our share of highs also.

Chapter 21

I kind of feel as is I'm well beyond the years I've lived on this earth because I've been dealt some hell of hands. As they say, what won't we do when our backs against the wall. I tried to stick to the mind frame money over everything. But it is easy for one to get trapped inside of the illusional life that the streets offer. In my days, I've witnessed all types of things. But where we live, the code is see no evil, hear no evil, and speak no evil. That applied to some because others were clearly doing the most. I guess 2Pac was right, 'To live and die in Delray.'

Telray is it's official new name, or maybe it's

been that from the start. After all, there are levels to this shit. The gift with me was once I saw something, I picked it up instantly. Me and Fruity began to hang more. We had been friends since me and my mom moved there. She was older than me but it seemed backwards like I was the oldest. She had a boyfriend that she was dating and she had just found out she was pregnant I was so happy for her. She was home cleaning, cooking, and playing house while I ran the streets on a paper chase. We barely spent as much time as we used to. So whenever we had the time to catch up, we would vibe.

With me, it was always one obstacle after the other. Why couldn't my life be like the fairy tale endings I only read about. Instead, I'm living front and center like hey batter-batter. The game was good to me so I had no complaints. I was eating and eating well. The game was no different from another because at the end of the day, we had our ups as well as our downs. When we had droughts it rained and it poured. I became more orchestrated with my shit. I had different teams that played different positions, so all I did was call shots and collect.

It finally felt good to me after putting in so much work. I was now in position to make shit pop. When you achieve power, the cockiness rears it's ugly head always causing confusion within the camp. I look at this shit like the government. I feel at times like I'm in combat. After all, this is America. Why I have to be a soldier? Let me be fucking great. Things were flowing too smooth. I smelled the shit. Certain shit never bothered me. I went unfazed about lots of things and I guess that's where I lost my footing and didn't catch the rug sliding from under me.

There are times that we lose sight of what's really in front of us. That saying there surely shall follow me all the days of my life and in what other area to apply it than the game.

Chapter 22

My dawgs wanted to hit the slab and run it up; if you know what I mean. At first, I was hesitant. But then worry went to the wayside and all I could imagine was the G's I would be holding. In my mind, my job was to carry on my mom's legacy making it to the finish line with a job well done. My outlook and perspective became damaged at an early age; leaving me to deal with dilemma after dilemma. Nevertheless, sticking to the plan to trap on the road was all that was on my mind.

I snapped out of it once again reflecting upon the past. I can remember so vividly the day I went to see my mom at the hospital. It was God making me aware that there was something totally wrong. I lived right around the corner from the hospital at that time. So, I walked what seemed the long green mile. It was the craziest day of my life. That's how God works though. He channels in to our six senses to alert us that there's danger around the corner. I was so confused and afraid there was an eerie feeling all over me. It was hard for me at first and then it dawned on me. I could only depend on me, that's why my view of the game became so clear. I had not been depressed lately. But whenever I felt overwhelmed, I would cloud my thoughts with the positive things and the fact that my mom still lived inside of me. They can never take her away because she is forever in my soul. She will forever live inside of me. It's times like this that make me appreciate my brothers. I couldn't imagine having to live in this cold world all alone.

Funny how the roles have reversed. Now it was like I was the mother instead of the sister. I never knew I could fulfill so many roles with me being just one person. That's living proof that God is good and he will never put on us too much for us to bear. We were all going through it. We were just dealing with things in our own ways. Sometimes I get so angry. I strived to be able to take care of all us. Between my aunt drinking and me and her fighting, in my mind all I felt like I had were these streets. It was crazy that I found love amid the devils playground.

The road trip was coming up so my focus was on securing the bag and living my caviar dreams. We moved in complete silence and there was absolutely no detection of the fraud, so we were able to walk away unscathed. We set that shit all the way off. We were the real out of town pie flippers. We are the true definition of highway goons, with the exception of being all chics. Who said that a woman can't do a mans job? I strongly disagree because I am proof that a woman can do a mans job and she can do it better. I'm just keeping it real or at least trying to anyways.

Once we began dealing with a certain amount of

cash, the ride became tricky. See this is where we have to pay attention. We can't stand up dead sleep. We had to keep our eyes on the prize. Whenever money was involved, you would see the true meaning of friendship. Money is the root to all evil. It was written.

Chapter 23

Since I clicked up with the chic from up top, we had been on some major move type stunts. I was knee deep when the petty sideways ass issues popped up. Fruity had been throwing me shade. Now I was trying to figure out what was the beef for? For the life of me I couldn't find out what was tea when I was the one that put her up on some shit. But that's how it went when a bitch pretend to be your friend. When in reality they are really your enemy. I started to peep the flaw shit when it came down to some cash. One thing I don't do is play about my funds. I will shut me some shit down immediately. I saw people lose their entire existence right in front of me. So I never underestimate what a bitch ain't plotting to do.

I kind of distanced myself to be rid of the fuckery. I clearly had no time for that. I was never on the same type of time as them is what they hated. Each little crew that we broke down into did good. We all made major moves and always stunted. For example, me and my god sister always showed up and showed out. They hated to see us coming and coming together. It was mad fake love, but we played the opposition. Like we do, we did us. Them hoes can't stand us. We are some boss bitches that demand our section.

Me and sis began flexing on them and showing how to ball. It was automatic beef. That's when the underlying shit hit the surface and the game gets grimier. But when that currency involved, a bitch will cut your throat. I get the game from Ole G. She my goodie. She stood by me and showed me real love when I needed my mother. She was the missing link that appeared like an angel in disguise; sent to heaven especially for me. It's weird more so than crazy because it was as if I lived two lives. So, I was caught in between two worlds. Don't get me wrong with my Goddie, we swerved on any event. It's always flexing season over there. That's what we do. That's why I say that this hustle shit is in my bloodline and it runs deeper than average. It's like I carry a confidence within that just can't be knocked and that's how I roll.

I had a lot going on at this time. Goddie was like, "Man check this out. All you have to do is leave everything in the past and live a whole new life; where it was always big things popping."

The entire family welcomed me wholeheartedly and we did so many memorable things together. See my Goddie never struggled. She was blessed beyond measures and she was also smart. She achieved anything that she put her mind to and she was on top all the time. She inspired me to become better and she also showed me how young women take care of themselves. I love that lady. She means the world to me. She makes sure I'm always straight and does a lot for me. She loves me like her own daughter. I'm blessed beyond measures. Here I am chasing the game and fame when it gets delivered to me personally on my very own silver platter.

Chapter 24

I was off the scene for real at times because it was too much. The way them bitches was acting about the money, had made me feeling like we weren't a good team anymore. So I planned to break off and do my own thing anyways because I was the supplier and had all the workers anyways. So what I needed them for? That was my exact question. When I came back through, I was going to be moving a different way to throw bitches off the trail.

Mean while, I got very comfortable enjoying my Goddie and her big plush half a milli crib, deep down south. Dade is where the ballers ball. It was beautiful. Everyday was fun and excitement. I finally got to feel what a life without any worries felt like. Trust me, it was a new feeling that I loved every second. It was easy living that lavish lifestyle. Affording all of the fancy accessories that came along with having bread. I mean it was sweet. Each car in the garage was foreign. BMW his and BMW hers. Yacht down at the marina, RV equipped to carry a family of four.

My Goodie had opened a business; which actually ended up becoming successful. She brought a plaza and one of the suites became a hair salon. It was the fanciest in all of Miami and she was definitely living her best life. I enjoyed being at the shop around Goddie watching her accomplish her dreams. She gave me even more ambition than I had in the beginning because now I no longer have to dream. I'm living a reality that many only dreams of. I mean don't get me wrong, everybody doesn't want to see another person doing better than them. They want you to be on their level, advance never;

or at least that's what they dumb ass thought. The lifestyle that I'm living can become addictive fast because you get accustomed to living a certain way. It's like the rich black folk version if I may say.

I was in no rush to get back to Telray where the haters hate and the snakes lay and wait. It was kind of like me looking at life through a different lens. It almost seemed real until I realized I was just a pawn in this game we call life. I was shooting at the wrong version because this was chess not checkers. Lately, I had been really considering elevating and creating a new path; which could eventually take me out the game. In my hood everybody hustled but we just all hustled for different things. We all had our own agendas. So once we broke bread, everybody did them. Where I come from, if we don't move our feet, we don't eat. So it's kill or be killed.

Lately it seemed as if everything was moving to a better accord. So in actuality, I was more at peace being incognito. I felt like there should be times when I could relax and just really sleep on life. I mean rest and relaxation was starting to become the new me. I was never the conceded type. I mean, I like what I like and that was pretty much my attitude. If it did not pertain or was relevant to me, I missed it. You know if it doesn't apply, let it fly.

My mind was on chill mode. So there was no grind or hustle. That was the very best part of being blessed. My thoughts were transforming into positive affirmations. The sun was shining bright and I saw myself changing. My friend kept inviting me to stop by her new place and check her out. I been missing in action and even she will not let me be great. After all, I did value our friendship. We kind of went through a lot together as our friendship grew. Whenever we chilled, it was all love; positive vibes. I plan to see her as soon as I get back in the area to see what she really got going on.

Chapter 25

The more time I spent around Fruity, I could see that she was very manipulative when it came down to boys; whom we thought at that time were men. Fruity had several baby daddies and she walked around as if she was the shit. I know that's right. Without self confidence for yourself, a nigga damn sure ain't gone respect a real bitch. That's just how this shit went. I learned first hand. It was what it was. These niggas are really for everybody. I always kept that wall up to prevent the pepe because I was trying to make cash and live. Not let a nigga drag me. I was the only one doing the dragging around here.

I planned to get up with ole boy tonight. So I went above the norm and reserved a room at the Embassy Suites so that I can make my fantasy a reality. He had no idea what was in store for him. I hit him up and sent him the official booty call. Of course, he was game. I arrived at the room early with my toiletries in tow; preparing for the wild night ahead of me. The closer it got to the time he was coming, I caught butterflies. For some reason, I was very jittery. Either way, it was going down. So there was no turning back. He was on time and so was I.

When he entered the hotel room, he was surprised. The entire living room was decorated with rose petals and candles. The jacuzzi was filled with Caress Pomegranate. That was my personal body wash. It smelled so damn good. I opened the door for him, dressed with only my robe and bedroom shoes on. Little did he know, I was naked up under the robe. Once he scoped the scenery, he followed my lead and we both stood by the jacuzzi.

Slowly, I untied my robe and let it fall from my shoulders. I was completely naked. We stood face to face as if we were having a stare down or even similar to that of a gun fight. Awkward to say the least. He began to unbutton his pants and remove his clothing. I starred at him in disbelief that this moment was actually occurring. He was working with a monster and he knew how to work it. This is the moment I yearned. We must've made love all night. It was so sweet and passionate. I could do this forever. That was how he had me feeling.

From that day, we were practically inseparable. Wherever he was, I was. I thought that my girl would be happy for me now that she saw me developing a relationship with someone that was just as into me as I was into him. But that's when I noticed the change with her attitude. I did not like the vibes that I was getting. I let Beaver know how I felt about how she was acting and he said, "Don't trip. Ain't no pressure. It's us against the world." So I said fuck the world because all that mattered was me and him; not the next bitch.

I gathered my clothes and told Fruity that I was going home but I went to Beaver house instead. We continued what we started and nothing else mattered at all. Our bond was becoming stronger and I was falling each day, more and more in love with him. I never really knew much about Beaver being that we were from two different cities. He lived in West Palm Beach and we never ran in the same circles. I asked a few people from around his way about him and everything checked out to be gate. So I felt even more at ease. We were together 24/7 and I wasn't making any plans to do anything else.

I needed to make a play run up a check real quick. "Bae I gotta go handle something." I told him.

"What's wrong." He asked. There wasn't anything wrong. I just needed to secure the bag. He was hesitant but once he knew I was coming back, he was chill. Since I got back, I was on some other stuff; which took all my time up. I was in need of cash. I hit my friend up and we shook life. That was just the break I needed. Now I can go back to laying up.

My friends were now all saying something. Everyone was complaining about my absence. It was so crazy because all I wanted to do was lay up. One of my friends said, "Friend, I hope your ass hasn't gotten pregnant."

"What?" I frowned. That threw me. Pregnant! Where did that come from? My mind went back to all the hours, days, and nights of love making I was having unprotected. Pregnant never crossed my thoughts. I got scared because having a baby was a huge responsibility. We were young and we were in the streets to heavy. I told him that night to get condoms and that was the very first time he ever blew his top on me. That didn't work out well at all.

The next month my period was late and time was flying so fast I never realized that it never came the entire month. I told him that I thought we were having a baby. "What?" He was so happy. It made me excited so we scheduled an appointment for the pregnancy testing. We were both stunned and speechless we were expecting. That was a huge game changer. I am going to be a mother. This was a first for both of us. His family was so caring and accepting. I knew that this was all apart of Gods plan.

Chapter 26

Everything was starting to move rapidly. There were rumors speculating that my nigga and his click had ran off in some big time dealers crib at gun point, straight laying them down and jacking them for all the loot. Things were too hectic for me because now that I was an expecting mother to be. I couldn't afford to let anyone or anything come between me and my first unborn seed. This shit was throwing me. I needed to smoke but ole boy had began putting down. So there was no smoke. I wanted all the smoke. Ain't this about a bitch! I didn't know what to expect. It was as if was clueless as to what types of moves this nigga was really making. I knew he was on plays but I had no idea this type. Shit like this gets you killed from my block. So I can only imagine what niggas of this caliber may be willing to do. In the game there were just certain rules that could not be broken and if they were broken, shit got real ugly. That's when the consequences and repercussions rear their ugly heads. At this point, I'm completely confused more so afraid if anything. The sad part is this nigga playing dumb about the entire situation.

I went to sleep with all types of wild thoughts running wild in my illusions. At this point I'm thinking I should just take my ass home. At least there I know I'm safe to let my guards down. These niggas silly these days. They walking around smoking all types of shit and will do whatever it takes to chase that next high. I looked at drug addicts as people that are just so lost within themselves; that they basically just give up all hopes and surrender themselves to that monkey on their back. I can never wrap my thoughts around the place in their life that has brought them to the bottomless pit. I guess some shit I just will never understand.

The next morning I woke up early, showered and began to get dressed. When suddenly he rolled over. "Bitch where the fuck you think you going!"

I didn't even know exactly how to respond because for starters I was not a bitch; his, nor anybody his else's. Secondly, how dare he treat me as if I'm his child. I may have been his baby's mother, but he had me all fucked up and he was about to muthafucking know it. I turned around on the edge of the bed and rolled my neck so got damn hard, that bitch was about to pop off. Then I cursed him the fuck out.

"How dare you fuck nigga try me like this! Bitch you must be out your mind because I am not any of your other hoes! I'm that bitch and I refuse to let or any other nigga disrespect me. Bitch I'm done! I'm going home!" I jumped off the bed damn near tripping. That's how quick my reflexes kicked in. I was pissed the fuck off. Like big mad, big facts. This bitch lunged forward so fucking fast. I thought this nigga was apart of the tiger family. He slung me on the bed and leaned his weight down over me; staring me directly in my eyes without blinking and boldly spoke.

"Bitch you ain't going no where! I will kill you! You're mine forever! Ain't no getting out."

Somehow I felt that. It echoed throughout my entire being. In my head I'm asking myself what the hell have I gotten myself into. To top it off, I'm pregnant with this crazy ass nigga baby. I better execute a strategized plan to escape. Shit! I can't go home. That will be the first place he will look. Damn, I gotta think and think fast. He was exhausting me. Now that I was pregnant, the smallest shit irritated me.

Suddenly all of his home boys were around more and they were always talking softly as if everything was bugged. Almost to the point of them whispering faintly. I may not know everything, but I knew enough to know that there was some shit in the kitchen that wasn't clean. Lord I just had to get me and my child out of harms way. This wasn't going to be an easy obstacle but maybe the friends hanging around more can give me the lead way I need to break camp. I had no one that I could call to confide in. I hadn't been making moves so therefore my money was funny. To top it off, them hoes started throwing shade when me and ole boy locked in. It was as if they wanted him or that's how I felt anyways because real friends would never let a nigga come between them.

He started to pay extra attention to me more like me being monitored. But what could I say or even do? All I could do was play along and act like everything was fine. That was the hardest part because its so hard for me to pretend. Either way, I was fucked because it was all bad and there wasn't a damn thing that I could do to change things. He had me right where he wanted me. Now I'm beginning to wonder was this all apart of his plan to lure me in and take me down.

All of my clothes were starting to get too small. My stomach began to protrude so now there was no hiding the baby. I needed to go shopping. So I used that as the perfect excuse to leave. But wouldn't you know he was prepared. He said, "Come on baby! Let's go." He drove me in his car to the plaza up on Palm Beach Lakes. There was every store imaginable there so I had me a field day at his expense. We were going to buy some things for our baby but we didn't know the gender. So we figured another time and another place. He must've been tired because I sure was. We walked the entire outlet it seemed.

When we headed to the parking lot, we saw some chics in a black Honda behind the car trying to peep through his windows. He had real dark limo tints. "Here we go."

I just knew that one of these hoes was going to say that they were fucking him, but they definitely didn't. I guess the expression on my face spoke for me. They said the dumbest shit in the world. "Oh my bad. I thought this was a car that I knew I'm sorry."

Now if that's not suspicious what is? I looked at

him with uncertainty and of course he said nothing. We sat in absolute silence for what seemed like eternity and then he said, "So when are you going to stop trying me. I know you fucking that nigga. What? Is it his baby? I see the way y'all give each other eye contact."

"What the fuck! Nigga you got to be out your fucking rabbit ass mind." I wouldn't dare fuck his friends. Not one of them lame ass niggas. We were cool but that was that. Where the fuck is all this coming from? I had no damn idea just how crazy this shit was about to get. The more I thought about what he had said, the madder I became. "I got to get away from you! This is not going to work. I can't live like this. I refuse to."

"Bitch try me! You ain't got a choice." He yelled.

Instantly, I began to vomit. "Please pull over. I don't feel well." I felt like a had a massive head rush. He had brought me so many clothes, underwear, bra's, pajamas, shoes, and toiletries. I might as well pushed going home or getting away out of my head because that wasn't going to occur anytime soon. All he wanted to do now was fuck and the sex was the bomb. But he had become so overprotective it was to the point I almost wanted to turn down the dick; if that fire head wasn't a part of the package. Mind blowing it was by far the best I had ever had. I guess I had to fake it until I make it or at least that's what I convinced myself of.

Being that this was the first relationship I had, I really had no idea how to handle his ass. But trust me, I was catching on faster than he thought I would. It was funny to me because I was the one that really had the control. I was the one he wanted and I wanted him so badly as well. But so much had happened in such a short time. I was a little unsure of how things would pan out. The less drama I had, the better off I was. That was for sure. I knew that if I knew nothing else. I felt at first like I wanted this and I still do feel that way at times and other times I feel like I made a big mistake. My head was all fucked up and he was loving every minute of it. As long as he respected me, we would never have any problems. He let them hoes know who mama was and in my eyes, that was all that mattered to me.

Chapter 27

It had been about two months since all the shit escalated. Now I'm getting as big as a house and our relationship is flowing a lot smoother. I can actually see myself doing this. The one thing I could never figure out was why does love give me so many mixed emotions. Was it my hormones that kept me all over the place or was it a nerve problem? I'm still trying to find out.

Tomorrow I have my sonogram appointment so we would finally know what we are having. I can't lie, ever since I found out I was pregnant, I wanted to give him a son. What man doesn't want his junior? A legacy to carry on all his beliefs, morals, and values. Now that we were finding out, I was anxious.

It's a girl. I guess he put that dick down on me and I couldn't even resist his thrusts. I could only surrender my love to him. Now I'm stuck thinking about her name. I had about four more months to get right. At that very second, it was as if every ounce of fear and doubt went out the window and all I could see was me and my family. Ain't that funny how love will do us? Love can make us do right and it can make us do wrong. I was a little upset when I found out I wouldn't be the first to give him a junior. But then I thought all daughters hold the keys to their father's heart forever. So I was still winning.

Now that I was further along in my trimester, I began planning accordingly for the new family edition. I was shocked that I was really about to be a mother. I can still remember when I announced my pregnancy to the family. Everyone was happy. It finally began to feel as if things were going to be better for me. So I had a lot to look forward to. My friend was well connected. He knew people that knew people. He pulled a few strings and landed me a brand new apartment on the far side of the complex. It was in the building where the two bedrooms were. I had a lot to do while I still felt motivated. This was my first child. This is a very special occasion for me.

Having a daughter is a privilege because there were so many themes and characters to choose from. I was a barbie fanatic as a child. My Goddie was glad that I was stepping up; even if my place was in the projects. She came through and broke bread. She furnished my entire crib. She did that lacing me up from one store. She got me a black leather, three piece sofa set, with matching tables, lamps, pictures, vases, a stereo for the living room and dining room table. I was set. I did the bathroom and added my feminine touch; wallpaper, curtains, rugs, and etc. When it was complete, it was hot. I cleaned up daily. Pregnant and all. There was nothing I loved more than the smell of fresh bleach and Pine Sol.

The baby room was decorated with the crib and the toddler bed. My baby daddy went all out. This was his first also so he made sure we had the best. He spoiled me and made me think that things would remain this way forever. We shopped damn near every day. We had so much baby stuff. The room was literally on go. There was everything for a little girl under the sun. Goddie ain't make it no better. She was ready for the baby to come. She went to the warehouse and brought cases of baby hygiene, pampers and wipes. I was so blessed.

Now we all were waiting on our new arrival. Times like these made the love seem so real. My baby daddy and I made love all day long. He made sure he fed his daughter and his baby mama. I was loving it and before I knew it, I was so deeply in love with this nigga. He had no idea that he was stuck for life. We talked about our daughter name and we couldn't agree. I guess we would cross that path when we cross it. I was too busy lamping in my best life. My brothers were extra helpful. They were there for me and they couldn't await their niece.

They were looking forward to being uncles. At least my baby would never be harmed because she had two uncles that would die and go to the depths of hell about her. That was a blessing because I ain't have any big sister to protect me and keep me safe.

Beaver and I were closer than ever. Our relationship was deeper now than I could've imagined. These were the best days of my life and I was truly happy. I stopped doing anything so Beaver was taking care of all the bills and me. I wanted for nothing at all. One day out of the blue, Beaver came home and gave me ten thousand dollars to put in my savings account. I wanted to ask questions about where the money came from but something inside me said, the less I know the better off I am. He did a lot of things in silence so I never knew what he was up to. I just knew he was collecting our coins. Yeah I say ours because me and my baby were gone be alright and he was going to make certain of that.

All I wanted to do was continue preparing for the arrival of my princess. Everything else pretty much got put on the back burner. I hated the morning sickness because every morning for at least three months, I was throwing up. My digestive system changed drastically. Here I was the type of person that would eat just about everything. There weren't too many foods that I didn't like and now all of a sudden, I had to watch what I ate. This shit made me mad because it took me so long to feel better. My baby was healthy. She was growing fine inside her mother's womb and there weren't any issues that put us in danger. So my pregnancy has been great.

I could tell the way Beaver acted that he was really excited to become a father. Although we were young, we weren't the average teenagers by far. With me losing my mom, this pregnancy was at one point delicate for me because all I could imagine is what if my daughter had to lose me. I let the fear of death plant negative seeds knowing that there was nothing I could do about death. When its our time, we got to go. I recall grandma saying that we were born to die and she would always talk about it as if she wasn't afraid to die. I guess not after living so many years, we all die. That's the wickedness of the world that plagued us with the curse of death. I just looked at life different and I knew that there were going to be changes for me. Being that I had a daughter, I could never let anything or anyone harm her. I would die before I let that happen.

CHAPTER 28

My thoughts were all over the place because there were things that were required of me as a mother and there was also the bickering that me and Beaver would do. I hated when we argued. It made me upset. I once had to be admitted into the hospital for them to monitor the baby. I worked myself up to the point that I was dehydrated mentally and physically. When we weren't getting along, I would leave to let everything die down. But that seemed to stop working since he thought that I was sneaking to see someone else. Boy was he crazy! Here I am, big and pregnant from him, live with him, and fucking only him and this nigga has the nerve to question me. I never questioned him when he was out all time of night; when he should've been home with me. Anything could've happened. I could've went into premature labor but was I stressing him? It was as if I couldn't breathe on my own. He had to be the one breathing for me.

At least when the baby is born, he will have something to do that keeps him busy and I can breathe a little. My friends wanted to throw me a baby shower but I didn't want one because I had all of the stuff I needed and some. They wouldn't settle for no, so they insisted that we have the shower. It was so pretty the way they decorated the room. They rented a banquet hall that was large enough to fit a capacity of 350. Of course the shower wouldn't have more than twenty guests. I'm thinking because I doubt if my aunt, Goddie, or Beavers grandparents will want to come. We all have done it all so the baby wasn't in need.

So many fake friends came to see the layout; you already know. My girl did her thing. The colors were pink, purple, and silver and she had everything on beat. That girl knows she can decorate. I keep telling her she needs to become an interior decorator. She got skills. But she was too busy chasing fast money. The decorating business was too slow for her. That's how that fast cash was. It had an adrenaline rush that you just kept chasing.

Beaver never came. He doesn't like the girls anymore and he barely allowed me time to kick it like we used to. It's like everything went to the left when we found out about the baby. He became overprotective. I never had that much attention; especially from a man. So now that I had it, I was overwhelmed. They say we should be careful what we ask for and I guess that's the truth.

*****

Down to Dade and enrolling in the community college. It all sounded good but how would that work for me and Beaver? He was already all on me. He wasn't going to let me move away with the baby.

Then I had my girls wanting me go hit a lick with them. I thought that would've been good being I ain't hustled for the past two months. My dawg, she found out she was pregnant. So she needed some baby stuff and I wasn't doing shit. So I rode with her to hit Babies R Us. Shit, all I did was walk around and look at the baby stuff because I had all mine already. She was over there doing her thing. She started walking from the clothing section to where I was by the car seats. "Lets go." She said. We began walking towards the exit both in tow. As soon as we neared the door, I saw this dude walking towards us. I kept walking and he grabbed my dawg. She tried to resist. All I could do because it happened so fast was run to the car and speed the fuck off. Shit, he scared me. I am pregnant and I wasn't stealing. Lord, what was she going to do because he had her. She was going to jail.

Damn Beaver told me stop doing that shit and here it was, my dawg got cased up. Fuck! I was hot. I had to wait for her to call me and let me know the deal. She definitely had to post bond. She was my dawg. I would help her out if she needed help. It took what seemed like hours for her to be transported and processed. Finally, she called.

RING! RING!

"Hello!"

"You have a collect call from Jamie. From the Palm Beach County Detention Center. To accept, press five. To block any future calls from this person press eight." I pressed five.

"Bitch what the hell." I said.

"Dawg that was crazy right!"

"Hell yeah it was!" I agreed. She told me they charged her with robbery and petit theft. She was good though. She did the bond. She was waiting to be released. She needed a ride. "Call me when they let you out and I will scoop you." I lived right around the corner from the jail so that wouldn't be an issue. She could count on me to pick her up. Damn she in all this trouble and she pregnant too. I was starting to get spooked. I didn't want Beaver to know that I was with her. He would never let me hear the end of it and he would not let me pick her up. I knew that I had to keep quiet or he would snap. I was already put on edge once today so I was chilling.

I couldn't understand how my dawg didn't have all her baby stuff when she hustled every day just like me and she had no bills. She lived with her grandma and she had no car. Where the hell was her money going? It wasn't adding up. I tried to mind my business because if a bitch ask me any questions, its gone be a problem.

Beaver and I went to Red Lobster and ate. Right when we were getting into the car, the phone rang. It was my dawg in jail. If I don't answer it he will swear that it's a nigga. Fuck rec blowed. I had to answer and act dumb because he was literally reading my lips as the words came out. "Babe will you take me to pick up my dawg?"

I was saved by the bell. Before I said from where, he said, "No, I have to run. I am getting into my car. You pick her up and drop her off. I will be back home by that time."

Thank the Lord his messy ass ain't get a whiff of

that tea because he would've been on my ass like white on rice. My dawg wanted to smoke and I of course stopped smoking. So she had to get her own weed. She had me to drop her to a nigga house that she was fucking with. I guess she was staying the night there because I clearly had to get home and get showered for bed. I began acting like an old lady; that's what pregnancy does for you. I wasn't real lazy but I had my moments. I did lots of walking and I ate healthy. I love fresh fruit from Publix. I craved certain things and Beaver was right there catering to me and his first born seed. Life for me couldn't be any better.

I made it home and started the shower. When I finished, I threw on my robe and went into the kitchen to get a snack. My fat ass. That's what I did late at night; ate like crazy. You would've thought I was still smoking the way I ate. But it was the baby eating. I grabbed my snacks and got in the bed watching TV. I must've dozed off because when I awakened, the TV was still playing and the morning sun was breaking through the dark curtains we had up to our window. I looked over and Beavers spot was empty. He ain't come home.

"What the fuck?" I jumped out of bed and marched into the living room. He wasn't there either. I opened the front door and his car wasn't in the driveway. Now this is strange. I call his grandma and she picks up immediately. She was so upset she could hardly talk. I couldn't understand the words that were coming out of her mouth. "Mom, calm down. What is wrong? What is going on?"

She managed to let out, "He got shot." That's where I passed out. Next thing I knew, I was woke laying in a hospital bed inside of Bethesda.

"How did I get here?" Is all I was thinking. That's when I looked over and saw Hazel. She was right there and she was so distressed. She told me that after she told me that Beaver had got shot. I fainted or blacked out and she sent the paramedics to my apartment. All of this was news to me. I wanted out of this hospital bed and I wanted out immediately.

I looked over and she said, "Baby you must calm

down. They are monitoring the baby's heart beat because when you passed out, there could've been a possible lack of oxygen."

"Where is Beaver?" I asked.

"Take it easy baby. Everything is going to be all right."

That was no comfort. I began to yell and become enraged. The last thing I remember was the nurse shooting something into my IV. Who knows how long I was out before I woke up and I asked the nurse can she get the doctor because I had to leave the hospital. The nurse said that she would go and get the doctor so that he could talk to me.

"Excuse me. Would you happen to know where my baby daddy is at?" I asked.

She didn't seem to have any clue what I was talking about. Now ain't this a bitch! I am in the hospital and I don't know what happened to Beaver. I have to get out of here if I have to sign myself out! Straight up. All of my thoughts were of him and where he was or what happened to him. I have to get up out of here asap. I jumped out of bed and began dressing. I had to go and they were only slowing me down. I had to pick up the pace and get there. I felt it; Beaver needed me. I called a cab escaping from the hospital by hiding in the restrooms until the taxi arrived to haul me off.

As soon as I stepped foot inside of the taxi, I blurted out the address; "506 Erie Place. Get me there." The taxi turned on the meter and of course began the drive there. As soon as we turned on Erie Place, there was Nanny out there bleaching and scrubbing the driveway. Her face was a stone cold, hard, skinned glare that made me think the worst. The cab stopped and I over paid him so I could get out and get to the bottom of things. Here it was I am, six months pregnant and this nigga could be dead. How can I bear child to a father who is dead from birth? This is the craziest shit ever. Nanny turned around and saw me inside the taxi and she threw down the water hose and held her hands on her hip. Now all I could do was stare her down while hoping and praying that my baby daddy was still alive. This nigga was crazy most definitely but he was my heart and he was all that mattered to me at the time.

Once inside Nanny told me that Beaver was in surgery as we spoke at St. Mary's. Of course I was in route. When I made it there, I was already tired as fuck. I had been up since 7:30 this morning and it was damn near noon. I registered at the hospital and went up to the surgery waiting room and waited until I was informed that he was out of surgery and now in his own room. It was as if my heart shattered all over again. This was the one thing I truly dreaded. No matter what we went through, we had that hood love that stood the test of times. It was times like these that I really appreciated the love that we shared. Regardless of how we were living, in my eyes we could do no wrong. I was a real bitch and I was his bitch. I would be the very first person he sees when he comes to.

Usually on normal mornings I am always sick with the morning sickness. But strangely, today I was fine. Our daughter was a soldier for sure because she wasn't bending at all. She was riding for her ole boy. I was finally allowed into the room and there he was laid out in the hospital bed with a hospital gown on; sleep still. I guess he was heavily medicated so he was still drugged. They had an officer guarding him. His right ankle was shackled to the hospital bed post with a handcuff. When he finally shook life, I was right there sitting in the same spot I sat in when I entered the room hours earlier. It was almost dinner time he was drowsy and he called me. My heart dropped and I fell in love with him all over again. Our love story was so real and true.

"Yes bae." He moaned as he reached out for my arm and I walked closer to the bed. He grabbed my hand and caressed it gently. We both stared into each others eyes getting lost in one another. There were no words spoke, only eye gestures. "Bae you need to eat."

The officer was pretty nice and cool. He respected the fact that we were black young parents. Although Beaver was in jail, he still was a human being. I ordered us all some KFC, and I fed Beaver the mashed potatoes and shredded pieces of chicken. With the officer being on the scene, we couldn't speak about anything at all. I wanted to know what had happened and who did this to him. He had lied to me in the past about many things but I felt that his lies were only to cover up the foul shit he done in them streets. I didn't give a fuck what at this point. I wanted to know who hurt my baby. This went on for almost a month. He was tied to the hospital bed while his pregnant baby mama was out there running the streets heartlessly. I got that lawyer money up and he had commissary. He was straight. All I needed him to do was heal so that our family could be ok.

Once we got the lawyer, things fell in motion and he was home before we knew it. The baby was that much closer to being born. I had saved all of the cash he accumulated along the way and every dime that he gave me, was accounted for. So he had no reason to resort back to the streets. We had an egg nest. I learned that from Goddie. She was the one person that showed me that a woman is the head and at the end of the day, she does whatever she has to in order to provide for hers while protecting hers.

When I thought back about my grandparents, they were always the ideal couple in my eyes. I. hindsight, they were the couple that lived within their means, and held a simple yet loving life. Then there was my mother and my father whom I knew very little about and can literally count on my one hand the times we spent together. That was not the way I vision my daughter being raised without a father. I wanted more than ever for us to have an ideal relationship. But hell, we were young still and our whole lives were in front of us. I just hoped that I made the decision to love him the way he loves me. It was too late now because we were parents now and I only awaited the days that he would be able to profess his love to his girls; me and our daughter. I knew deep down inside that he loved me. He just was lost inside the streets. He had childhood pain that followed him throughout his life. I tried telling him about his so called friends and the lifestyle that he was living but who was I to check him when I was living on the wild side too!

Lately, I had began to gain a different perspective about things and now I saw clearer. Beaver ended up getting house arrest for the charges they had on him. He was breaking in peoples houses while they were home sleeping; stealing all of their valuables. I had no clue that this was going on so of course he said very little and I asked even less. That's the way I looked at it because he was so sneaky and all he did was lie to me about the pettiest shit. We spent more time at home than ever and it felt so good knowing where my man was at night. The feeling of reassurance that required no calling or texting all night, tossing and turning until he slid the key in the door. I remember them nights and don't get me wrong, I never felt like he was with another broad. I was more so concerned about his well being. That was the difference between me and the rest of them hoes. They were artificial and I was 100%.

Even while I've been pregnant, all the niggas

been still hollering at me. I ain't lose my juice. I still got it and that pissed Beaver off more when he expected me to look like shit. But he forgot I am still the shit. I be laughing so hard on the inside when he be acting all jealous. I find that very amusing. All I did was sit in the house and ate all day then I slept the rest of the day away and stay up late watching all the movies. That gave us something to do but it sucked because I couldn't smoke weed anymore so I couldn't be extra high. I was watching Beaver and he had no choice but to move differently. But I knew in my gut that he was up to something and for his sake, I hoped he wasn't. His wounds hadn't even healed properly and he was still running wild. I told him about being sneaky because them people gone catch his ass and when he goes back to jail, his ass wont be able to get out and my money wont be going to that raggedy ass jail. He thinks that I wont be able to live without him but he has another thing coming! Baby or no baby. I will always be in position to win. I am a boss and he knows that. I guess all my pesturing paid off because Beaver found a job so that made me happy. He is always trying to convince me that he is doing the right things. But I keep telling him it's not me he must convince. As they say, what's done in the dark comes to the light. So I would say I will sit back and enjoy the ride and let whatever is be. Now that Beaver was working, we had more family structure. So when he got off, we had family time and I loved it. I had become spoiled to the attention he showered upon me.

Made in the USA
Columbia, SC
13 April 2025